NO GREATER LOVE, NO GREATER LOSS

ISHA JOHNSON
© 2016

Isha Johnson
SheDopeLLC@gmail.com

For information about booking, or special discounts for bulk purchases
please contact the author at the address above or visit
www.nogreaterlovenogreaterloss.com.

Library of Congress Cataloging-in-Publication Data

Isha Johnson,
No Greater Love, No Greater Loss: My Pain Revealed
Published by: SheDope, LLC: Fayetteville, NC 28314

Library of Congress Control Number: 2016916414

ISBN: 978---0---6926946---5---7

10 9 8 7 6 5 4 3 2 1

Printed in the United States of America

Note: I have tried to recreate events, locales and conversations from
my memories of them. In order to maintain their anonymity in some
instances I may have changed the names of individuals.

Dedication

In recognition of **LIFE**, **LOVE**, and **STRENGTH**, this book is dedicated to my beautiful daughter,

Danasia.

Without you, Danasia, I simply would not be here today.

Everything I do is for you, so that you will have a better future and so you will live a better life than my own. You may not understand my decisions, but everything will have been worth it, if you never have to endure my struggles in your own life.

My *LIFE* is amazing because I have your love and support, Danasia. Our bond is like no other. You are what every mother imagines a wonderful daughter to be; and I love you with each breath in my body.

To my wonderful daddy, Isiah, you were the first person to teach me how to *LOVE* others, yet also love myself. I can only hope that I am still making you proud and that you are smiling down as I make it through all the things people didn't think I would or could.

I love you, Daddy.

Last but never least, my precious angel in Heaven and my **STRENGTH**, my son Jaquel; you empower me every day. It is because of you this book even exists, but how I wish it never had to be written. Everything about you made me strong, Ja. You are my firstborn, my first love; and because of you, I have found a strength that I'd never even imagined possible.

We will never forget the special little boy that stole everyone's heart.

~ I LOVE YOU, Ja. ~

* CONTENTS *

PROLOGUE

As I walked into my son's room, something just didn't feel right. I hadn't heard the usual 'morning sounds' that my son had always made on every other day, those predictable and familiar sounds that signaled the start of a new day in our home. I realized my son hadn't even turned on his cartoons or run into my bedroom to see if I was up yet. My back stiffened a bit, and I held my breath, as I walked into his silent bedroom. His tiny form was underneath his bedcovers and he didn't stir in the least as I walked closer. It was odd for him to sleep so late. He was usually up early and eager to start his day of play, cartoons and laughter.

"Ja? Baby?" I said, as I pulled back the covers with a shaking hand.

He was still wearing his blue and white two-piece pajama set with long sleeves and long pants; but my son was totally still, so unnaturally and eerily still.

"Oh God! Ja! Baby, wake up! Ja!"

As I picked him up, I realized my sweet little toddler was stiff as a board. His tiny pink tongue hung awkwardly from his mouth and toward the side of his soft, little cheek.

"Junior! *Junior!*" I screamed, as I looked down at my son's stiff, still form. "Call someone, Junior! Hurry!"

"Um, what's wrong?" my husband yelled back from our bedroom.

"Get help now! Call for help!"

Moments later, Junior walked into Ja's room, as I shook my son and desperately tried to wake him. My whole body trembled and my chest was tight with pain, like a dagger had pierced my heart. Tears ran from my face and I could barely breathe.

"It's busy," Junior said from the doorway in a dull, monotone voice I'd never before heard from him.

"Busy? What? What're you talking about? 9-11 can't be BUSY!" I screamed, as I took steps toward him, and then snatched the cordless phone from his hand as I held my son close to me.

Seconds later, as the phone shook in my hand, I heard '911, what's your emergency?' in my ear.

"My baby!" I screamed. "My baby! He's gone! I need help! He's... He's not breathing!"

"Ma'am, your baby's not breathing?"

"No! No! He's GONE!" I wailed as I still awkwardly held Ja's stiff body against mine.

"Alright, ma'am. Take a breath and listen to me. I want you to do CPR," the calm 911 dispatcher told me. "Place the baby on the floor. Do it now. I'll walk you through it. Come on now. Hurry."

Junior stood silent in the doorway and watched, like a silent observer, as I laid Ja onto the carpet in his bedroom, beside some blocks and stuffed animals.

"Open his mouth and make sure it's completely clear and that there is nothing in his mouth," the 9-11 dispatcher directed with her practiced voice of calm. "Okay now, place your mouth over both his nose and his mouth and then give him two full rescue breaths; and then I want you to do begin chest compressions. Go ahead. Do it now."

Ja's tiny tongue was still hanging haphazardly out from his bluish-gray colored lips, but I frantically did just as the dispatcher had instructed. I blew into his cold, little mouth and willed him to breathe as I silently prayed in desperation.

Please, God! Please! Help my baby to breathe! Help us, God!

Just as I'd given him life only a couple short years ago, more than anything, I desperately wanted to give life to my tiny son in that horrific moment. My body shook and my tears fell onto my son's still figure, but my efforts didn't seem to be working. As I desperately did more chest compressions, and then more full breaths,

Junior looked down on me; but my husband never moved closer nor offered to help me.

"Ja! Come on, baby! Breathe! Please, God! Make him breathe!" I wailed, like a wounded wild animal, as my tears continued to drip onto my lifeless baby's face and his pajama shirt. "Please! Ja, please! Breathe, baby! God, help him breathe!"

I knelt over my little son and focused even harder, alternately on breaths and then chest compressions, careful to do them both correctly. Nothing seemed to work, no matter what I did. I'd have given anything, even my very own life, if only my son would take a breath.

"Oh, God! Please, God! Help me!" I wailed.

Chapter 1 – End of Innocence

The day had started out like hundreds of other ordinary days. A friend had told me about a case lot sale at our base's local commissary, and so I told her I'd join her and take advantage of some savings while stocking our pantry.

"Let's go and get our nails done too, while we're out," Kerry had suggested.

"Yeah, okay," I agreed, laughingly looking down at my hands. "These nails could definitely use it."

After we went to the commissary, and stocked up, I stopped back by my house to put away the groceries I'd bought on base.

"Hey! Where are you going *now?*" Junior asked, with an air of irritation, as I hastily finished putting away the cold foods into the freezer and refrigerator.

"Just to get my nails done over in Dothan. I'm sure we won't be that long."

"So, let me get this straight. You expect for me to stay here with both of these kids, while you're off getting your nails done?" Junior snickered. "Really?"

"It won't kill you, you know? I never go anywhere, Junior. What's it matter? You can watch them for a little bit. You'd be here anyway."

15

Things hadn't been good between Junior and me for some time. In fact, it had even gotten so bad that we were already moving toward divorce. It was just a matter of time.

A little while later, while Kerry and I were at the nail salon, I got a phone call from a friend who was also my Army recruiter.

"Hey, girl!" he said. "What're you up to today?"

"Just getting my nails done in Dothan."

"I'm in Dothan right now too," he said. "Why don't you come by and see me and we can catch-up?"

"Well, I'm with my friend," I told him. "And we just decided we're meeting some other girls for drinks later."

"Have your friend drop you off here, and then I'll drive you home later; and your girlfriends can pick you up at your house when they're ready."

"Yeah, okay, that'll work. I'll see you in a bit."

I called Junior, got his voicemail and left him a message that I'd be out a bit longer and that I was going to see my girlfriends for a drink later.

My recruiter, and I visited for a couple hours and we got caught up on everything going on in both of our lives. He then drove me home, as he'd promised. As we drove along, my cell phone rang and I immediately saw it was Junior.

"Hey, when are you gonna be home?" Junior demanded. "I want to leave and go out with some friends too, you know! You can take these kids!"

"I'm on the way, Junior," I said, exasperated with my husband's childish and insistent attitude.

"Isha, where are you anyway? Oh, never mind! But if you're not here in ten minutes, then I'm leaving the kids here and taking off! You hear me?"

Just as I hung up my phone, my friend turned his car into a gas station alongside the road.

"It'll just take a minute," he said. "Sorry."

I smiled and looked down at my watch. The thought of my two children, left all alone, absolutely terrified me. My son was a toddler and my daughter just a baby. Anything could happen if they were left unsupervised. I tried to tell myself Junior would never leave them alone; but the truth was, even I wasn't sure anymore. Things had been strained between us for so long and I didn't know

18

what he might do, especially since he felt that he'd been inconvenienced and put upon.

Minutes later, just before midnight, my friend dropped me off at my home, located on Fort Rucker Army Base. I was relieved to see Junior's car in the carport of our side of the tidy duplex where we lived in base housing.

"Thanks!" I hurriedly said to my friend, as I rushed from the car, intent on getting inside as quickly as possible.

As soon as I got inside the house, I saw headlights pull up outside and I remembered my girlfriends were supposed to come by to get me and go out for a drink. I stepped outside again, and met them just on the other side of the front door. I didn't want them to witness my husband and   the scene he might make.

"Sorry," I said, "Junior is making such a big deal of it. I guess I'm not going now. Maybe next time."

"What? Are you kidding me?" Kerry said. "C'mon! You can go out for one drink!"

"No, it's not gonna work now. Sorry."

As I quietly shut the door behind me again, I turned around toward Junior.

"Go on and go out!" I told him. "You wanted to go so bad, so *go*! Go on!"

"I'm not going out anymore."

"What?" I asked, irritated with my husband by this point. "You pushed for me to get home! Why not? Why aren't you going out now?"

Junior just turned away from me and walked into the hall and toward our bedroom.

"Where are the kids?" I asked.

20

"Sleeping. They're both asleep."

I went down the hall to check on the kids, and first stopped in our daughter's room. She was fast asleep in her crib and I pulled her blanket up around her.

I next went into my son's room and turned on a small lamp.

"What are you doing?" Junior asked from the doorway at the hall.

"Checking on him," I whispered.

Satisfied that Ja was sleeping too, I turned off the lamp and walked out of his room. I didn't want to be anywhere near Junior since I knew we'd most certainly only argue and I'd grown tired of it. I called my girlfriend to see if she could come by and pick me up for a few hours, to allow Junior time to fall asleep.

"Well, he's changed his mind for some reason," I told her. "I don't know why, but now he's not going out, so I guess I will."

My friend said she would text me before she came by; and that it would be a little while before she could get to my house again.

"I think I'm going out after all," I told Junior. "We obviously can't *both* stay here."

Junior was in the bedroom and I didn't want to have to talk to him further, so I went to the sofa to lie down for a little bit and wait for my friend's text. I closed my eyes and almost instantly drifted off to sleep in the quiet house.

The next thing I knew, I heard the sounds of Ja's breathing coming from his bedroom. He'd recently had bronchitis, so I got

22

up to go into his room and check on him. I looked in at my son and he was still asleep, so I went in my darkened bedroom.

Junior was in our bed, but he was still awake, even though it was nearly 3am.

"Hey, what were you doing?" he asked me through the darkness.

"I was checking on Ja. He's breathing funny, I think he must still be sick. We need to take him to the doctor in the morning. I guess he's still got bronchitis."

"Yeah, okay. Right," Junior agreed.

I didn't even change my clothes, as I climbed into bed. I hadn't heard from my friend; and I figured she was having a good time and couldn't come back for me, though it didn't matter. I was tired anyway. I just put my head on my pillow and fell right to sleep. The next time I opened my eyes, the sun was up and our baby daughter was in bed next to me, and pulling my hair.

"Really? Are you just gonna let her pull my hair like that?" I asked Junior, as I unwound my hair from our baby's tiny fingers.

Without a single word, Junior moved our daughter away from my hair as I rubbed my burning scalp. I realized the house was strangely quiet as I glanced at a nearby clock that read 10:00am. On any other Sunday morning, Ja would already be up and out of his bed, happily watching *Barney* on TV. That is, unless he'd wet the bed during the night, which usually meant that I'd find him in his bed, shyly waiting for me to come in and help him.

"Hey, where's Ja?" I asked Junior. "It's so late."

"Still asleep, I guess," he quietly answered.

"No, not *this* late," I said as I got out of bed. "Well, maybe... if he wet the bed."

The house was so still, so unusually quiet, without the sounds of Ja playing or watching his favorite program on TV.

"Ja? Baby, are you up?" I called as I walked into his silent bedroom.

Chapter 2 – In an Instant

The next few minutes are still a blur, and quite honestly, something I wish my mind would allow me to forget altogether. I've heard it said that women 'forget the pain of childbirth,' but I felt certain that the kind of raw, searing pain that came next would forever be etched into my very soul.

When the EMS workers finally arrived, I was still kneeling over my son on the floor and still wearing the clothes from the previous night.

"Ma'am," one of them said, as he put his hands on my shoulders to push me aside. "Ma'am, you've got to move. Let us take over."

I couldn't though. I couldn't make myself move away from my baby and just leave him there, still and quiet on the floor.

"No! No! No!" I wailed. "Oh, God! Noooo!"

"Come on now," the other EMS person said, as he took me from the other worker's grasp and then nearly dragged me away from Ja and then from his bedroom.

My mind raced as I tried to figure out what to do next. I thought I might vomit or faint. I didn't know what to do and I could barely breathe. I first stepped left, then right, and finally I went to grab my cell phone and immediately called my daddy in New Jersey.

"Hello?" he answered. "Isha?"

"He's gone!" I screamed as my knees went weak and I sunk to the floor. I was on my knees in the hallway near the bathroom. "He's gone! He's gone!" I wailed.

"What?" Daddy asked in a panicked tone. "What is it? Who, Isha? Who's gone?"

I couldn't even form a word, much less a sentence through my heaving, gulping sobs as I sat on my knees on the floor and fell forward to the carpet.

"Isha, what's wrong?" My daddy again asked. "What's happening down there?"

I don't recall what I said next to my daddy. Even today, I'm still not entirely sure about what happened next and it's all a fog; but maybe that's a merciful gift that the mind gives us in the midst of more pain than we can possibly handle.

I saw that the police were talking to Junior in the living room. Holding the doorframe of the bathroom door, I pulled myself up and tried to go toward Ja's room. Life seemed to move in slow motion and I couldn't make out the words people said. My head ached, my stomach felt queasy and the floor and the walls seemed to sway with a sickening lurch that made me feel unsteady.

"Ma'am," someone said in what sounded like a muffled drone, "I'm sorry, but you really can't be in there?"

Another pair of hands was on my shoulders and they pulled me from Ja's bedroom and guided me down the hall. It felt as if the hands, not me, made my legs move. I didn't feel like I could walk on my own.

"Here you go," a voice said. "Sit here."

People rose up all around me. I felt paralyzed and unable to move or speak as I sat on a chair while chaos flitted about all around me. I was sure I might vomit and that I could never make it to the bathroom, though I didn't care either.

Strangers were all over my house and people were telling me I couldn't go to my baby, *my own son*! People took photos and wrote on clipboards and spoke in hushed tones; and then I heard a voice clearly say 'rigor mortis has already set in.'

"Give me my baby!" I screamed, as I leapt up, rushed down the hall and tried to push past the man that blocked Ja's bedroom door. "Give him to me right now! I'm his mother! Give me my baby! Let me help him!"

"No, ma'am, we can't do that," he said, as he put his hands on my shoulders to hold me back from my son.

"Here, come this way," another man said from behind me. "Let's go outside for a minute. Come on now."

My stomach was nauseated, the room swayed and my chest ached even worse. It was as if I'd been caught in some horrific nightmare, but I couldn't wake up to make it all stop.

As I went outside, guided by a pair of unseen hands, I saw that my girlfriend had arrived. She was holding my daughter in her arms. A police officer took me by the elbow and led me closer as he firmly held my arm, so I couldn't turn and run back inside the house to my son.

"Can you take her and her daughter over to your house?" he asked my friend. "We need to get her out of here."

"Where is my husband?" I demanded of the officer.

"Well, we need to talk to him for a few minutes. We've got some questions for him," he replied. "You just go with your friend right now, and take your daughter with you."

The whole scene was surreal and as if it were happening to someone else as I helplessly watched the sickening nightmare unfold. It was Sunday morning. We were supposed to be having breakfast. The kids should be in their pajamas, happily chattering and watching Barney on the TV.

What's going on? What is happening? I thought as my friend helped me into the front seat of her car.

Junior and I had first met in Advanced Infantry Training. I'd been Active Duty Army at the time, and he was in the National Guard. We were both learning our respective jobs at that time. Later, after I had left the Active Duty, Junior then decided to go Active and I went into the Reserves. So, as my whole world spiraled out of control on that Sunday morning, our orderly life was entirely upended.

For what seemed like hours, I sobbed and sobbed nonstop, choking and hacking gulping cries that sounded like a wounded animal. My friend, whose husband was also a soldier, took care of my daughter at her house, since I could not. I tried to make some sense out of what was happening and I wondered where my husband was and why he wasn't coming to get me or even to check on me.

I lost all sense of time, as different people tried to talk to me. My NCO came to my friend's home to speak to me, but I couldn't begin to carry on a conversation. All I wanted was my baby, back in my arms, cuddled close against me, and safe from the world and whatever had taken him so cruelly from me. I wanted to feel his warmth snuggled against me and I yearned to breathe in his sweet scent again and hold it inside of me forever, safe from the reality of what was happening.

People came and went as if my friend had a revolving door on the front of her home. The faces and voices changed, though I couldn't focus on any of them. Everyone looked at me with pity and sadness in their teary eyes; and my own tears never stopped. Friends, and even strangers, tried in vain to get me to eat; but I didn't care if I ever ate another bite of food again. I just wanted my son back! Food could never satiate the hollow void inside of me. It wasn't what my soul craved. Besides, I was so filled with pain that there was no room inside me for hunger or food and I felt sure there never would be again.

It felt like I was trapped in a blurry nightmare where nothing was clear and nothing could possibly be real because it was all too awful to even be happening. The conversation around me was like white noise with a constant whirring, buzzing sound, but still nothing made sense. The faces of all the people were out of focus and nondescript. My eyes hurt from crying and my stomach ached; but worse than anything, my heart ached for my son. There was no real sense of time and it felt as if I just *existed*, trapped and drowning in the bizarre confusion all around me.

Junior's parents also eventually appeared through 'the revolving door' of my friend's home. I didn't know anyone had called them, but I heard someone say they'd driven up from Jacksonville, Florida. They'd come to the house because Junior was finally at my friend's house by this time and his parents had wanted to get to their son.

A couple days after my hellish nightmare began, and I know this only because I figured it out later, we finally got some news. The CID, or Criminal Investigation Division, had made sure someone stayed with me at all times as they watched me like vultures, just waiting for their prey to weaken or die; so, of course, they were with me when the call came in. They'd been mere feet away from me from the moment I'd left my home, with their accusatory stares and judgmental looks. It felt like they waited for me to finally crumble and drop to the floor, so they could pick the carcass of the horrible mother whom they thought to be a monster who'd taken the life of her own child. Their stares and their attitudes told me they'd already decided that I had hurt my own precious son. It sickened me that anyone could think I was capable of such a heinous and unforgivable act, especially against one of my very own children.

I was at the dining room table in my friend's home when someone handed me the phone. Junior sat slouched in a chair across from me at the table and another person was seated in the chair between the two of us. There was a bucket of fried chicken on the table, the smell of which had seriously nauseated me; yet I was too weak to get up and move from the table, where everyone kept trying to coax me to eat something. It was the prosecutor on the phone line and he said he had some news for me.

"We just got the autopsy results back, Isha," he explained, "And Jaquel's death was definitely not an accident."

Not an accident. Not an accident. The words reverberated in my mind, bouncing off my brain and slamming into my skull, again and again, as if inside a sickening pinball game. My brain refused to absorb and accept the words. I couldn't focus on anything the prosecutor said after that. *Not an accident! Not an accident!*

"Nooooooo!" I screamed, as I dropped the phone and dissolved into sobs. "Nooooooo!"

Even as I wailed and sobbed, I thought there had to be some misunderstanding or some other explanation for what had occurred. I knew that I had certainly not harmed Ja and that Junior had never hit either of the kids. It was all so confusing and sickening at the same time.

Junior's head was in his hands, as one of the CID people walked over and placed a hand on his shoulder.

"We'll have to take him now," he said to no one in particular.

"What?" someone said. "Take him? What do you mean?"

"Oh my God!" I screamed at Junior through my sobs. "What did you do? What did you DO?"

He didn't even look at me as he robotically stood up and then followed the CID people outside of my friend's home. Junior was by now crying too; but he didn't answer me, and he still wouldn't look at me, as he silently walked outside, followed by two Army people and a CID investigator.

Minutes earlier, I'd have sworn that my world couldn't get any more horrific, and yet it just had. In an instant, the prosecutor's phone call began my descent into a hell like I'd never known or even imagined possible.

Chapter 3 – Alone

Most wives expect that their husbands will be at their sides during a catastrophic and life-changing event. My husband though, was being held at the barracks on the Army base and he'd been placed under suicide watch. Junior had been arrested later the same day, after I'd received the phone call from the prosecutor.

There would be no reassuring hugs, supportive words or empathetic looks from my husband. In fact, I wouldn't see Junior again for some time, until I eventually went to visit him in the prison in Pensacola, Florida where he was held.

Even though people surrounded me, I still felt so very alone, frightened and vulnerable as I navigated through my nightmare. Junior and I had been married for a year, and we had dated for a little less than a year before I had married him. When I'd found out I was pregnant, I decided to marry Junior because Ja, my baby, didn't have his father in his life and I didn't want the same for Junior's baby that I carried. It had seemed like the responsible thing to do, and the main thing that the Army had taught me was how to be responsible. I thought I was doing the right thing.

My mind played over all sorts of scenarios about what could have possibly happened to my son. Each one made me sick, and I couldn't imagine that Junior had physically harmed my sweet baby boy. I knew though, that things had been tense between Junior and me for some time; and that Junior wasn't happy that I'd asked him to watch both of the kids on that fateful Saturday.

I even chastised myself for going out and leaving the kids with Junior, because I never really went out that often; and so it had been unusual for me to do something at all with a girlfriend that day. All the 'what ifs' constantly plagued me and I so desperately just wanted to turn back the clock and go back and relive that life-changing day again so I could do things differently. I wanted to wake up on that fateful Sunday morning to the sounds of Ja happily playing; and I wanted to walk out of my bedroom to see his smiling face. But I was cruelly trapped in every mother's worst nightmare, the loss of her child, her firstborn and her first love.

Junior sent me a steady stream of handwritten letters from the jail. I could tell from his writings that his emotions were still all over the place. He went from professing his love on one day to wild, hurtful rants on the next.

My heart ached for my son, but I also had my daughter to think about. She needed her mother, especially since her father was gone and her big brother was forever taken from her life. It was such a lonely time for me too, with my baby gone and my husband gone and accused of taking my son's life. The prosecutor had begun to work with me in his attempts to build a solid case against Junior; and I still couldn't wrap my head around the possibility that my husband had most likely killed my baby. Sure, Junior and I had been headed toward a separation; but still he'd never been violent, not once; and so the whole thing seemed bizarre and entirely incomprehensible to me.

I knew I'd take my baby home to New Jersey for his funeral, but it seemed hard to believe; because at 21, I'd never even been to a funeral. It sickened me to think I'd be taking my son back to where my family lived – in a tiny casket. My parents talked with me over the phone from their home in New Jersey.

"We're making the arrangements," my mom told me. "We thought it

46

would be helpful to get these things done. We'll see you tomorrow when you get here."

"What? You guys did the arrangements? Oh, yeah, okay, I guess," I said distractedly, as I watched my little daughter happily play, unaffected by the permanent change in her world.

She'd never even get to know her brother, never play with him, and never have him as her best friend. I'd never watch him go on his first date, graduate high school, go to college or get married. I'd never get to see his first child and watch him become a father. My whole world had been so violently shaken, like a snow globe; and I had no say in any of it, as the disturbed, broken pieces fell all around me.

"You ready, Isha?" Kerry asked, as she grabbed her car keys from the nearby   tabletop.

"What? Oh, sure," I said, shaken from my thoughts.

She drove me back to my home so I could pack a few things for the trip the next day for my daughter, Danasia, and myself. A few minutes later, I stepped back inside my home, now still, quiet and cold without Ja inside of its walls.

"Come on now," Kerry said, as she took Danasia from my arms. "Don't think about it. It's too much. Just get a few things and let's go."

I couldn't care less what clothes I grabbed from my drawers and my closet as I stuffed clothes, shoes and toiletries into a suitcase. I then went into Danasia's room and grabbed some of her things too. As I walked past Ja's room, I stopped to pause and look into his still, silent room, the place he'd taken his very last breath.

"Come on now," Kerry said as she placed a hand on my arm to tear me away from my thoughts, as my daughter happily chattered and laughed.

How I wished I could be unaffected and untouched by the hellish reality like my daughter seemed to be. She was so innocent, free and happy.

Kerry and I put my suitcase in her car's trunk and then I took my daughter from her to place my baby in her car seat. Just then, cars came from all directions and sped toward us and braked, blocking us in my driveway. It was like something out of a TV drama, as the cars pulled in and parked at all angles in my yard and driveway. I buckled my daughter into her seat, and watched in shock as uniformed and official looking people got out of the cars.

"What the…." Kerry began.

"I'm sorry Mrs. Johnson," a woman said, as she came closer, "But due to what's happened, we're here to take Danasia into custody."

"What?" I asked, as I reflexively stood in front of the car door, the only barrier between my daughter and the people who threatened to take her from me. "What are you talking about?"

"I'm sorry," the woman continued, "But the state says that when one child dies in the home, that we have to take the other children out of the home. It's just a precaution, a formality really. I've got the paperwork here, if you'd like to see it. It's a state order, signed by a judge."

"Ma'am," a man said, "Step aside so she can get the child."

"What? No!" I said, with tears in my eyes. "You can't take my daughter from me! I've done nothing wrong!"

"I'm afraid we can," the man said, as he put his hands on my upper arms to nudge me aside.

The woman opened the car door and Danasia cried out in all the chaos and commotion. The man blocked me from reaching my baby, as I tried to get around him to get to her.

"No!" I cried. "You can't do this! I've already lost my son! Please! You can't take my baby from me too!"

As the woman held Danasia, my fear quickly grew into indignant anger.

"This is harassment!" I said. "You can't do this! You have no right!"

"We're following our instructions, ma'am," the woman said. "I'm truly sorry."

As the woman walked away with my baby in her arms, I sobbed as another piece of my heart was ripped out.

"Mommy loves you, Nae-Nae!" I called out. "Mommy loves you, Baby!"

Then, just as quickly as they'd all swooped in, all the official people and all their government-issued cars drove away with a piece of my heart. I stood there beside my empty home, with my heart just as empty.

My house was a shell that had once been wrapped around my family, and my body was just a shell wrapped around my crumbling heart. Both were painfully still, cold and hollow; and I wondered if either would ever hold joy and peace again.

"Come on, Hon," Kerry said, "Let's get you home."

Home? I thought to myself. *But I had a home. I have no home now, nowhere to belong, nowhere that safely holds my family and all that's important to me in the world. Home?*

Minutes later, after I'd composed myself, I phoned Junior's parents.

"Listen," I explained, "You've got to come and get the baby. She can't go to some foster home! I don't want her with strangers!"

Thankfully, Junior's parents came right away and we all attended an emergency custody hearing the next morning. After spending one night with strangers, my daughter was released into the custody of her grandparents; or her grandfather and her step-grandmother, to be exact. I knew Junior's parents loved Danasia and that she'd be well cared for by them, so that was of some consolation; but I also knew I'd have to deal with the hurdle of getting my daughter back too.

"We'll bring her with us to New Jersey for the funeral," Junior's stepmom told me. "So at least you'll see her in Jersey City."

With Danasia situated in the care of Junior's parents, I had to board a plane and fly to New Jersey the next day on the airlines' bereavement ticket. I'd also paid for a bus ticket for Kerry to get to the funeral, but I still had to fly alone.

It took all I had to get on that plane and stiffly buckle myself into the seat. I didn't want to speak to anyone, so I tried not to make eye contact with the nearby passengers. It seemed absurd to make small talk when my whole world had just been imploded. I didn't want a drink or peanuts from the flight attendant. I just wanted to disappear and have all the pain and hell go away. Still today, I'm not sure how I found the strength to physically keep going. Frankly, I'm not sure how my heart even kept beating in those days. I guess I was on autopilot, is all I can presume.

Chapter 4 – Judged On My Worst Day

When I got to my parents' home in Jersey City, I first went to my old bedroom to put my things down. There stood Ja's first crib, the one he'd slept in right after he'd been born. I'd still just been in high school, a young teenaged mother, when I got pregnant; and I brought my son home from the hospital only four months after graduation. I looked around the bedroom and remembered holding my baby, cuddling him, singing to him and watching him sleep peacefully in his crib. A pit formed in my stomach, my chest ached and I thought I might vomit.

The memories were just too much, too overwhelming. I turned around, picked up my bags and rushed from the room, leaving all the memories behind the closed the door – or so I thought.

"I can't do it," I told my dad, as I tried to shake off the feelings and all the memories. "I just can't stay here. I'm sorry. I just can't."

"It's okay," he said. "We understand. I've gone in there to look at his crib too. I know what it must be like for you."

I stayed at the home of a friend, just down the street from my parents' home. As it turned out, my mom had planned everything, every detail, for the funeral before I'd even arrived. In fact, she'd wanted to hold the funeral on a Saturday, but I told her I simply couldn't get to New Jersey that quickly with all that was going on. Maybe she thought she did what was best, but it irked me that I didn't have a say in my son's funeral and the way he'd be laid to rest.

I woke on the morning of Ja's funeral, Monday, September 22, 2003, with a sense of dread and an overwhelming gloom. Actually, to say 'I woke,' is not exactly the case, since I'd barely been able to sleep in the days after Ja's death. But on this day, it just didn't seem possible that I could be going to my own baby's funeral. I kept thinking 'parents should never bury their children. This can't be happening to me. It's not how it should be.'

The only redeeming factor on that morning, and the only thing that even got me out of bed, was my daughter, Nae-Nae. At least I could hold her close and breathe in her sweet scent as if to somehow mend the cracks in my heart and fill the void in my aching soul.

It didn't feel to me like I belonged in my old neighborhood, around my old friends and family, and all the memories of my youth. Years before, I'd grown up there; but those were very different times. In those earlier days, my mom had used drugs, shoplifted and often left me with her friends so she could go out and party. Her priorities were skewed, to say the least. Mom always knew that if she kept me with her while she partied, that I'd tell my dad about where she'd been and what she'd done.

Back in my old neighborhood now, I felt like my very presence was only a stark reminder to my dad and everyone else of those bygone days, and the bad times that they'd just as soon forget.

My mom and dad had split-up a few times when I was young, but then they always got back together. Mom had always been angry about something, about everything in fact – about life in general. She was just that kind of person; and wherever she went, chaos and anger also followed in her wake.

On the morning of Ja's funeral, I went back over to my dad and mom's home to get dressed. I just kept thinking 'how does a mother dress for her own child's funeral?' It just seemed surreal that I was even preparing to go and bury my precious son and say my final goodbye to the little boy who I'd brought into the world a couple years earlier. It felt like my body operated on it's own, autonomously; and with no input or effort from me as I watched myself go through the motions of getting dressed.

People hugged me and gave me their condolences, but there was an underlying tone of suspicion that hung over us, as if they wondered if it had been I who'd harmed little Ja and taken him from his life in this world.

I just wanted to scream at the top of my lungs 'I would never hurt my baby!' I saw the stares and sideways glances. It was exhausting and I didn't think I had the energy or could possibly muster the will to even reply to the insulting and sickening questions from people. I'd grown so weary from all the suspicion and innuendo.

"I don't know," I slowly said. "Really, I don't know either. I don't want to talk right now."

A little while later, as we rode in the back of the limo to the funeral, I felt the eyes of suspicion on me, even from my own family, from the very people who'd known me for my whole life.

How could they imagine I'd do such a thing? How can they believe such a thing about me?

My heart ached and my stomach churned as I silently rode along the familiar streets of my childhood. The distant memories of those times seemed so long ago. So much had happened in the years since I was a carefree teenager. I'd 'come home' to be with my family, during the worst time of my life; and the very people who'd watched me grow up and who once knew me best, now judged me with cynical hearts and critical eyes.

As the limo pulled up to the funeral home, I saw a sea of black all around the building that also spilled into the parking lot and across the lawn areas. Everywhere I looked, it was 'black and gray.' I didn't focus on any of the faces in the massive crowd. All I knew was that my little son lay inside the funeral home, wearing the all-white suit with the little jacket and slacks, in the tiniest of caskets. How I longed to hear Ja's voice, see his smile or feel his soft cheek on mine, even one more time.

My legs felt like lead as I silently got out of the limo with my daughter, my dad, my mother and Ja's godfather. I'd have blended into the sea of black, in my own short-sleeved knee length black dress, but the black ocean seemed too silent for me as I walked through the crowd. There must have been at least 100 mourners who waited to get inside the funeral home's chapel. It didn't feel like I was walking, as I floated or glided closer and closer to the door, not really wanting to go through it to meet the reality inside.

I'd realize later that so many people from my past had come to Jaquel's funeral. There were neighbors, old friends, people I'd gone to school with and distant relatives; and of course, there were relatives from Junior's family too.

My family stayed close as we made our way through the crowd and toward the open front door. I was almost numb until the very moment when I stepped inside the building. It was in that instant that the floodgates flung open wide, like the dam finally broke; and I wailed with primitive, guttural sounds like even I had never before heard.

My whole body wracked and heaved with sobs as I gasped, gulped and hyperventilated while my relatives tried to hold me up and physically support me. My body went weak and I couldn't stand, as my pain spilled forth like a tidal wave that threatened to wash away everyone in its path. The force of my agonized pain stunned even me and I had absolutely no control of it.

"Somebody call EMS!" a voice said. "Call 9-11!"

"We need to get her outta here!" another voice called out from somewhere nearby.

"Let's get her some air!" yet another voice directed.

My family helped me outside again and away from the crowd so I could get my breath and try to somewhat regain my composure. People handed me Kleenex, cold cloths and cups of water; until finally, I was able to breathe again as my body continued to heave.

"Let's go inside," I said, knowing I had to make myself go into the building before another wave of grief hit me like the second deadly tidal wave.

"Give your self a minute, Hon," Ja's godfather said, as someone dabbed my face with a handkerchief. "Take a few more deep breaths. Take your time."

A few minutes later, my family walked with me and we went back into the funeral home. When we entered the chapel, my eyes went immediately to the end of the aisle where my son's tiny casket silently stood. How I wished I were instead walking over to his bed to kiss him goodnight and tuck him in, safe and sound, and still here with me in this world. I still don't know how I made my legs take the steps that got me down the aisle and to the front of the chapel. It was no walk that any mother wants to have to make; and yet, in the weirdest of ways, no mother would decline to ever go to her child's side, even in the worst of times.

No one had gone up to Ja's casket yet, as they'd all respectfully waited, in order to allow me, as his mother, to first spend time with him. My uncle and Ja's godfather supported me and held me up, as I stood over my baby and looked down at his angelic little face that merely looked like he was peacefully sleeping. I kept thinking he should wake up and smile, ready to jump into my arms and happily play. As I gulped my tears and gasped guttural sounds, I somehow managed to place a photo of him, with Danasia and myself, into his tiny little hands before I turned to sit down in the front pew.

After I was seated, the ushers let other people walk up to the casket. All eyes were on me as people came into the chapel, but I didn't care. I felt their stares burn into my back. Whatever they thought of me in that moment made no difference to me as I settled my daughter in my lap, as she happily chattered and played with a program.

Ja's dad's family, one by one, eyed me with disdain and I felt their contempt, but I completely ignored it. His uncles walked past me with their fists tightly balled and their jaws clenched tight, as they gave me hateful looks that clearly said they thought 'I had taken my own baby's life.' Thankfully, my son's godfather and longtime friend of mine had seen this too. He walked over and sat down beside me in a show of silent solidarity and a clear warning to the men that 'this was no place for that sort of thing.'

My uncle then walked up to the men and quietly said, "I suggest you keep walking."

The behavior of Ja's father's family was shocking, since only a few weeks before, he had questioned whether Ja was even his biological child. I couldn't believe his audacity, but I guess it was his defensive reflex when he'd been asked to pay child support to help with his son's expenses.

Most of the funeral service was a blur as I just tried to breathe past the searing pain that bore through me. If breathing weren't involuntary, I feel sure I'd have ceased to even take another breath. It's impossible to convey a mother's pain when she's lost a child, her firstborn; but it's the closest thing to an actual death that one can imagine. In the moment, I didn't know that I'd have to learn to live again; all I knew was that the pain was nearly unbearable. It wasn't just emotional; it wasn't exactly physical; it was simply all consuming and overwhelming and it blanketed me head to toe and bore through me from one side to the other.

Words were spoken, music was played and prayers were offered, as I stoically sat and stared at the little white casket surrounded by white roses. Inside the casket lay a chunk of my heart that I'd have to learn to live without since I still had a daughter who needed her mother, who deserved her mother, since her father was in jail and charged with taking the life of her big brother.

When the main service had ended, we went next to a shorter graveside service. Danasia had to leave with her grandmother though, to get to the airport and board their flight back to Florida. It had been the smallest mercy to have her there with me, but saying goodbye to her was still unbearable. I'd lost one baby and the state had pulled away my other one from me.

There were clear skies and the weather was warm while everyone placed a flower atop Ja's casket, one by one. I crossed my arms and held my elbows as I cried, unable to even hold my daughter in the moment, since she'd been court ordered into the care of Junior's parents. It felt like my whole world had been shattered; and I was so very alone, as people, one by one, politely hugged me and said goodbye as I stood at my son's grave. Slowly, the sea of black disappeared.

"Come on, Honey," someone said to me, when there were only a few of us left.

"No, I want to wait," I numbly said.

As Ja's mother, I wanted to be there till the very last second, as my son was placed into his final resting place. Just like I'd have never turned away from him, and left him alone someplace, it felt like I couldn't turn and walk away from him here either. I'd have given anything to trade places with my baby, and to let him live a full life like he'd deserved. It still didn't seem like the nightmare could be real, and that my baby was gone.

Some time later, the black limo returned me to my dad's house. It was actually a two-family home and my grandma lived in the downstairs of the house. When I got back, I went upstairs to lie down and be alone – or even more alone than I already felt.

A couple hours later, I went downstairs. There was some mail on the kitchen table and I saw from the return address that it was from the state of New Jersey. I tore open the envelope and read the letter inside as I shook my head at the irony.

I've just buried our son, and here's this stupid piece of paper telling me what I already knew! I thought.

I called Ja's grandmother.

"Well, I got the results of the paternity test," I told her.

"And?" she asked.

"What we already knew!" I said.

"Oh, I already knew he was my grandson!" she confirmed.

Later that night, the accusatory stares continued. I saw the look in my uncle's eyes, so I just went outside the house with a few others. My uncle followed.

"Tell me the truth, Isha!" my uncle insisted, as he grabbed my arm. "What happened?"

"Are you kidding me?" I said, as I wrestled away from his accusatory grip. "*I* don't *KNOW* what happened! Believe me! I don't KNOW!"

But I could tell he didn't believe me. It was as if I couldn't just feel the horrific, searing pain of losing my baby. I had to also deal with all the questions, smirks and accusatory glances too.

Was it not enough for these people that I felt mortally wounded? Was it not enough that, if not for my daughter, I'd gladly lie down and take my own last breath, instead of living another day without my son? How can it be that these people are my own family? Isn't family supposed to support you, lift you up and comfort you in times like this?

Chapter 5 – Empty

Both my heart and my arms were empty when I returned to Alabama after my son's funeral. I felt like a hollow, cavernous being, empty and lost, as I navigated through life, just going through the motions. My son was gone; my daughter was in Florida with her grandparents; and my husband was in jail and charged with killing my son. I was alone as I drifted through my life, not caring about much, other than getting my daughter back with me.

I couldn't even go back to our house on the base, since the investigation was still ongoing. There was Crime Scene tape still up, all around the house, which told the neighbors and passersby that something awful had happened inside. By this time, stories and rumors swirled about, as everyone speculated on what had happened to little Ja. I saw the looks and felt the accusatory stares, even from strangers, who surmised that I'd had something to do with the death of my child.

Chelle's house offered a bit of privacy, even if her and I weren't the closest of friends. Kerry had dropped me there, with the promise that she'd come back soon; but I later learned that she was more interested in running around with her drug dealer boyfriend behind her husband's back.

Kerry and I had known each other from the Army Reserve unit I was with. I'd considered her a friend, although we weren't extremely close. Frankly, that was the only reason I'd bought her the bus ticket to New Jersey so she could attend Ja's funeral. I'd learn though, that people show you their true colors if you let them. After I'd returned to the base from New Jersey, Kerry became quite the gossip; and as if 'the truth' weren't sensational enough, she felt it her right to embellish her stories as needed. I soon learned that Kerry told multiple people that I 'hadn't even cried at the funeral,' which only made me look worse still to people who didn't really know me.

The CID investigators continued to harass me and they kept me under surveillance, as if I were a criminal. It hurt to think that anyone could even imagine that I could harm my own child; but what hurt even more was the raw, empty hole in my heart and the knowledge that my whole world had forever been changed.

I was so completely alone, as I waited for CID to conclude their investigation. Since I knew that *I* hadn't harmed Ja, it was clear to me that Junior was the one who had taken my son from me. It was a sickening realization and one I'd have never imagined could be a possibility. I wanted answers though; I wanted accountability; and I wanted desperately for someone to make some sense of all that had happened in the last few weeks.

Of course, I wasn't eating and I couldn't have cared less about something as insignificant as food. A few friends insisted one day that I accompany them to a Subway to get something to eat. As friends do, they incessantly tried to make me smile, even if for just a moment. Finally, just to make them stop *trying* to make me feel better, I forced a slight, closed-mouthed half-smile for maybe a second. I learned later that the CID investigators who'd followed me took my 'split-second accommodating smile' to mean that I didn't care that my son was gone. Since they were still in the early days of their investigation, of course they blew this whole miniscule moment out of proportion.

To complicate and confuse matters even more, Junior continued to write letters to me. His tone went erratically from kind and caring to argumentative and explosive. It felt to me like my whole world had imploded. I didn't have my son, or my daughter; or even the man I'd once taken as my husband.

Things between us hadn't been the best in the last months, but I'd never had even an inkling that my children might be in danger from Junior. But being left alone at Chelle's house most of the time gave me nothing but time to think. I mulled over the last months with Junior, our relationship and his behavior around the kids. I tried to find any clue, even the tiniest hint, that I might have missed that could have warned of what had occurred. I even let myself think of little Ja and what had happened to him. The questions swirled about in my head as I wondered what had occurred while

I'd been gone. My heart ached to think my son could have been hurt or frightened and that I wasn't there for him. These thoughts, in particular, were hard to even imagine; and I often had to physically shake my head to try and erase the images and possibilities from my mind. I preferred to think of Ja's big grin and his sparkling eyes that lit up a room. When I closed my eyes at night, I prayed that I'd dream of Ja and see his smiling, laughing face. Even when I did dream of him though, as soon as I opened my eyes, I was kicked in the stomach with the horrific reality that Ja was gone. My baby was gone and my arms were empty.

One day melded into the next, as I felt swallowed up by all that happened around me. It was as if I were a helpless spectator as I silently watched my life fall away, piece by piece. My heart ached to at least hold my daughter, feel her warmth and breathe in her scent that I missed so much.

Since the investigation into Ja's death was still ongoing, it was impossible to get Nae-Nae back, so she stayed with her grandparents in Florida. I couldn't even go back to our home and sit in her room and hold her stuffed animals because CID still considered our home to be a crime scene and so it couldn't be disturbed.

"You'll need to make alternate living arrangements," I was told. "You can't go back to live in the house."

I was finally able to get into another house on the base. While I had a roof over my head, that was pretty much *all* I had. The house was as empty as my heart with its quiet, cold walls and awful stillness.

"Can't I even get my furniture from our house?" I asked the woman at the base housing office. "I need my bed, a sofa, a table.....something!"

"No; I'm sorry," she explained, "But the house has been deemed a crime scene. Nothing can be disturbed until after the trial."

Junior had told the CID investigators that Ja had been jumping off some furniture earlier on the night he'd died. The only explanation Junior had offered was that Ja must have injured himself while jumping and playing. For this reason, the furniture could not be touched, moved or altered, since the forensics people needed to measure, document and calculate so the prosecutor could attempt to build a case against Junior. On the flipside, Junior's attorney might also use the information in his defense too to try and prove the theory that Ja had accidentally injured himself.

I was in a perpetual state of limbo, as I waited to get some answers about what had happened on that night. It was like time stood still and had left me in the middle of Hell, forgotten, alone and powerless, as I drowned in my pain and sadness. I'd have done anything to turn back the clock and live that life-altering day over again.

Chapter 6 – Learning to Live Again

I went to Florida to spend my daughter's first birthday with her. Chelle and her parents drove me to Jacksonville and dropped me off at Junior's aunt's home where I spent a couple days with Nae-Nae. It was far from the first birthday celebration I'd wanted for my daughter, but at least I was with her. It was also good for me to be with her because it forced me to care for her needs and interact with Nae-Nae.

While in Alabama, caring for myself no longer seemed remotely important anymore. There was no sense of time, and it was like I was trapped in a perpetual state from which I couldn't move nor escape. Eating wasn't important; sleeping didn't matter and on most days, I didn't even have the energy to take a shower. I'd just lie on my inflated mattress with the buzz of the TV in the background. The stress took its toll on my body as I lost weight and my hair began to fall out.

I looked and felt awful, but I couldn't have cared less. My arms and my heart ached for *both* of my children; and it hurt even more to know that I'd never again hold one of them, no matter what happened.

While in Florida, I tried to sound happy and upbeat around Nae-Nae. I didn't want her to feel my stress or see my pain and worry. I wanted to leave her with a 'happy picture of Mommy' in her mind. Still though, it pained me to know she'd never get to know her big brother and that her family had been destroyed.

Back in Alabama, my house couldn't have been further from a 'home,' with its stark, cold floors and empty walls. Since I hadn't been allowed to take my furnishings from our home, I had no furniture; and since I had virtually no money, it took until December for me to rent even a couple pieces from the local Rent-A-Center in town. On most nights, I slept fitfully, if it could even be called that, on my inflated air mattress. The silence was deafening, so I usually turned on the little rented TV in the living room, though I never really watched it. On some nights, I stayed at Chelle's house or with her parents who were so good to me.

I was in the house on base the day the prosecutor stopped by to talk to me. Chelle happened to be there too.

"We're formally charging Junior," he explained. "We've got enough to charge him with murder."

I nodded my head, but I still felt numb. By this time, I knew Junior must have done something to Ja. *Was it intentional? Was if officially murder?* It didn't matter to me. Either way, my son was gone.

"I have the autopsy photos," the prosecutor continued. "Do you want to see them, Isha?"

No, I don't WANT to see them! I thought, though I knew I had to view them. Everyone had continued to ask me about what had happened and what I knew, though I had no answers. Seeing the photos would make it all the more real, so I knew it was something I had to do.

"Are you sure?" Chelle asked me.

"Yeah. I am."

The prosecutor showed me the photos of little Ja, so still, forever still. I needed to sit down, so I took a seat next to Chelle on the sofa. The prosecutor laid out all the photos on the coffee table in front of us, one by one. He explained to me each of Ja's injuries and how they could have occurred. The aching pain welled within me mixed with a sickening disbelief that Junior could have done something so heinous, and to a tiny, innocent child. I had loved Junior. We had a daughter together. It seemed impossible.

"You are telling me," I said slowly to the prosecutor as I looked at Ja's images, "That my husband killed my child, my baby."

It was hard to even force the words out. Words like those should never cross a mother's lips. Quiet tears streamed down my face and dripped onto my shirt.

"It's what the evidence tells us, yes, ma'am. This is what Junior did to your baby."

Chelle tried to offer comfort, but there was nothing that could take away that kind of pain. The prosecutor didn't stay too long. Before he left, he reminded me that he'd like for me to testify against Junior at his trial. The photos had been the final turning point in my decision to testify. Seeing little Ja like that had pushed me over the edge.

As soon as the prosecutor had gone, Chelle suggested we go over to her house. For the rest of day, it felt like I was in slow motion as I numbly moved through the day. I just kept saying, 'How can this be?' as I tried to digest it all. My mind continued to see the awful photos of my son, as I wondered *How many times before had Junior harmed Ja?'* and *'Why didn't I see it?'*

Days later, Chelle stopped by my house to check on me and immediately she said, 'Isha, what is all this?' as she looked down at the floors with her fingers outstretched wide.

"My hair," I quietly said. "It hasn't stopped falling out. It's from all the stress, I think."

"Well, listen," Chelle said, "I've got a guy I want you to meet."

"What? I don't want to date anyone. Are you kidding?"

"You've got to get out of this house," she insisted. "Just come out with us one time. Just come and meet him and have a change of scenery. It'll do you good."

Finally, after much urging, I agreed to go and meet Chelle's friend, mainly so she'd stop prodding me. He was okay and he turned out to be a nice enough guy. In time, he even gave me some money to help me out, which I appreciated. I hated the place I was in, with no options and no choices, trapped and paralyzed. It felt like life was over and as if someone had pulled my whole life away from me and left me just barely existing.

"So what do you think of him?" Chelle asked me just before Christmas.

"Oh, I don't know. He's not really right for me."

What I really meant was that the guy was a drug dealer and I didn't want any part of that world. I had enough problems of my own without adding to them, so I soon broke things off with him. Nothing and no one could quell the pain or fill the emptiness inside of me, and I didn't need to be mixed up with someone else's issues.

After I broke things off with Chelle's friend, I took a hard look at the state of my life; and I took stock of what I had. Almost instantly, I realized that I had nothing; but I also realized that only I could change that fact and take back my life.

The feat seemed huge and overwhelming, but between December 2003 and July 2004, I had to literally learn to live again.

In January, I met Aaron, a nice guy who would soon become my best friend. Three months later, I started working again; but by May, I learned I was pregnant. Unlike my other two pregnancies, I didn't feel happy and hopeful for the future. Instead of sharing my news with everyone, I kept it to myself and was afraid to let people know I was pregnant.

What would people think? What might they say? Would I be the subject of rumors, gossip and innuendo? How could I possible tell people I'd allowed myself to get pregnant, with all that was going on? Would people think I'd tried to replace Ja with another child? Would people always talk about the new baby and scrutinize him or her? All the possibilities swirled about in my head and not one of them was good; and I constantly worried and lost more sleep.

It was such an emotional time for me. I felt entirely unsure and uncertain of what to do as I suffocated and sank in my life as it caved in around me like quicksand I couldn't escape. I was sure it wouldn't be good if I went into the courtroom pregnant when Junior finally went to trial. After much soul-searching, I finally made the decision to have an abortion. By the end of the year though, Aaron and I would eventually break-up.

Maintaining a relationship was simply too difficult at the time. My emotions were all over the place, I was focused on getting my daughter back in my custody and Junior was still facing trial. Whatever I was seeking was not to be found in a relationship. Broken and angry, I'd been constantly argumentative with Aaron, so he could never win with me.

How could he give me what I needed, when even I didn't know what that was? After we separated, Aaron and I were on again and off again a few times; but we eventually settled on being best friends.

Chapter 7 – Justice for Ja

As he waited for trial, Junior continued to send me letters. Each time I saw his handwriting, my stomach twisted in knots and my hands trembled as I ripped open the envelopes. The letters were always unpredictable and erratic, with messages of 'I love you' at the beginning and 'I hate you' at the end. Sometimes he wrote 'I miss my family' and 'RIP, Ja.' One day, as I opened an envelope, tiny cutout hearts fell out that had been torn in half, as if to represent Junior's broken heart.

*Yeah. You think **your** heart is broken?* I thought with no sympathy.

When Junior went to trial, my mom came from New Jersey; Ja's father and his own mom came and Junior's parents came too. They brought my daughter with them; and Nae-Nae also brought the only glint of happiness I felt.

Since the prosecution planned to call me to testify, I wasn't permitted to be inside the courtroom prior to my testimony. On Day Two of Junior's trial, I was called into the courtroom. Because it was a military trial, the courtroom wasn't a typical setting. An Officer of the Court presided from a long table; and the prosecutor sat at one table while the defense sat at a table to his side, both of them facing the Officer of the Court. People were seated behind the prosecution and the defense as they silently watched the trial unfold.

I walked into the courtroom when called and swore to provide truthful testimony. Most of the questions presented were about the day Ja had died, my whereabouts and what I saw when I got home that night. Of course, I had to also answer questions about the awful morning when I'd gone into Ja's room and found him in his bed; and how Junior had told me 'the 9-11 phone line had been busy' when I'd screamed for him to call for help. The whole thing was just bizarre and surreal as I went through the motions of answering the questions. It was as if I watched a sad movie, as an observer.

By Day Three of the trial, both the prosecution and the defense had rested and everyone awaited the ultimate decision of the Officer of the Court. We all waited in the hall, outside the courtroom, until we were eventually called to go back inside.

"We've got a decision," the prosecutor told all of us, as he held open the door to the courtroom that held Junior's fate and Ja's justice.

After we'd all gone inside and taken seats, the Officer of the Court spoke. My heart raced as I waited to hear the fate of the man I'd once loved.

"Based on the preponderance of evidence presented during trial, it is my belief that the defendant did not *intend* to kill the child. In order to have a verdict of murder, there must have been premeditation, which I do not believe existed in this case. How-e-ver...."

With that, the Officer of the Court stopped, looked at Junior, then cleared his throat and continued.

"How-e-ver, I feel sure that this child's death *could* have been prevented. The defendant could have gotten help for the boy and prevented his untimely and unnecessary death. For this reason, my finding is that the defendant is guilty of the charge of involuntary manslaughter; and he shall be sentenced for such."

There was a shuffling in the room as everyone digested the verdict in their own ways. While the finding relieved some, others were disappointed with the verdict. For me, I just wanted my baby back in my arms and I wanted the constant ache in my heart to go away.

"Sir," the Officer of the Court continued, as he looked straight at Junior, "This court sentences you to a period of 10 years in prison, with credit for one year already served in Pensacola."

There was no relief, no vindication and no sympathetic feelings. I wasn't sure what I'd expected, but I'd hoped for even the smallest bit of closure. It was instead like I'd been suspended in time, unable to move forward, since my life had been ripped away from me.

How does a mother move on with life when her child has been torn away from her? How can her heart even function when a part of it is gone? These were questions that plagued me.

These were the things that continued to keep me awake at night.

Still in the Reserves at the time of Junior's sentencing, I tried to stay focus on my job. My daughter was still officially in the custody of Junior's parents. It was such a difficult time for me. My life had been completely upended and tossed into turmoil. How I wished that I could go back in time and make the decision to stay at home on that fateful day that had changed everything.

As I tried to stay strong, I prayed, I talked to Ja and I often cried alone at night. It was also coming to light that some people whom I'd thought were friends, were in fact, not that at all. This reality would be another stab to my heart that would cause me to sometimes question people's intentions and motives.

After I'd heard that my supposed friend, Kerry, had been gossiping about me, I decided to confront her after I'd had enough. I knew she'd be at the Family Day event on the base, so I went looking for her. I wouldn't have even been there on that day, if not to finally confront the woman who'd been talking about me. The thought of happy family gatherings was, at this time, still the furthest thing from my mind. I had another girlfriend on my cell phone, Chelle, as I walked through all the families in search of the woman. When I found her, I opened the speaker on my phone, so the three of us could speak.

"Now tell me again where you got that information that you're spreading about my family and me!" I said to Kerry, as I looked her in the eye.

"It was Chelle!" she proclaimed. "Chelle told me!"

"You know I didn't tell you anything of that crap about Isha!" Chelle yelled from my speakerphone. "You're lying!"

When she saw the blazing fury in my eyes, the rail-thin, stick figure wisp of woman turned like a frightened animal and retreated like a jackrabbit that had just seen a coyote.

"I'll call you back!" I said into my phone, as I hung up and followed the frail woman running away from me as fast as she could.

I easily caught up to her panting, wheezing, sweaty form and grabbed her arm to spin her around.

"I don't want to hear that my name has even crossed your lips ever again! You're nothing but a liar!

Don't talk about my family or me ever again!" I yelled. "You got it?"

She couldn't speak, but she nodded her head as she wheezed and gasped for air. As I walked away, I felt sure she'd have passed out, and that it would be poetic justice if she did.

I learned later that the woman went to our NCO and asked for protection from me, which I must admit I found amusing. That incident was one of the eye-opening things that made me question some of my relationships with people.

When I'd married Junior, I had thought he was someone whom I knew well, someone who could be trusted with my children and a man who'd never do something like he did. After I'd lost Ja, I began to question many things.

The one thing I never questioned though, was my love for my daughter. It was my love for her that kept me going when I wanted only to give up after I'd lost Ja. Had it not been for Nae-Nae, I'd have had no reason to work through my loss and face the pain day after day of going on without my son. In an odd twist of circumstances, Junior had taken away one of my children, and yet he'd also given me another child that gave me reason to live.

Having Nae-Nae kept me moving forward as I navigated the hurdles and paperwork to formally regain custody of my daughter. Her grandparents took good care of her, and they surely love her too, but a girl needs to be with her mother. While I understood that Junior's parents wanted to raise her, I wanted her back in my custody. After all the endless paperwork, proceedings, phone calls and visits, I finally got Nae-Nae back into my custody in May 2005. As I held her and hugged her close, I felt a tiny piece of my fractured heart begin to heal.

Chapter 8 – Short Deployment

After I got Nae-Nae back, I felt like life was looking up. I tried to create as normal as life for us as possible. My job with Army seemed like a good fit for us at the time. Since I knew I'd have to deploy at some time, I setup a support system for my daughter and made arrangements for her care while I'd be away. It wasn't perfect, but this is a reality for enlisted men and women every day.

My daughter was like a ray of sunshine to me; and she was the one thing that kept me inspired as I worked to build us a life. As I met new people, I continued to tell them I had 'two children,' though I didn't share much more than that with most of them. Ja's photos were all around us and it was his smiling face and the memory of my son that gave me strength to do whatever necessary for Nae-Nae's happiness.

I lost my dad in 2007 and his death was a sort of turning point for me, I think. He'd always been my rock and the one person I could turn to in a storm. After he was laid to rest in the New Jersey cemetery, next to my son, I began to think about how short life can be and how important it is to live each day to the fullest. Like many people do at times like these, I began to consider my own mortality and the time I had left.

This was possibly the catalyst for what would occur in 2008, about a year after Dad had died. I'd gone home to New Jersey, and taken Nae-Nae with me, so she could visit with our relatives during the week of Thanksgiving. My younger sister, 10 years my junior, was so happy to see me that she nearly bowled me over as she ran to hug me when we arrived. In contrast to my sister's greeting, I noted that our mother didn't seem as elated to see Nae-Nae and me. It broke my heart to see my daughter treated as anything less than a treasured grandchild; and I resented that my mom doted over my sister's kids but almost ignored Nae-Nae altogether. I'd always tried to reinforce to Nae-Nae that she is a smart, strong and valuable person with so much to offer. My mom's indifference toward her wasn't something I could tolerate or allow.

Sadly, my sister didn't have the same relationship with our mom that I did; and she didn't fully understand my issues with our mother. To make matters worse, my sister and her kids also lived with our mom, so her opinions were probably slated too.

When Nae-Nae and I left New Jersey, I vowed that my mother wouldn't spend time with my daughter since there was no benefit to it. I felt myself growing stronger, as a woman and as a mother, and I knew it was my responsibility to keep my daughter away from toxic, negative people whose influence could harm her in any way.

It hurt me that my sister didn't understand my decision, but she saw things differently. Since I was 10 years older, I'd taken care of her when we were young; and I had even named her with the name 'Latia' when she'd been born. Since I didn't want to hurt Latia, I kept some things about our mom from her for several more years. It wouldn't be until the fall of 2015 when I shared details of why I wasn't a fan of our mother. I know that every family has their issues. I'm just thankful that I found the strength to make a decision about protecting my daughter from a relationship that could have, and probably would have, been negative and harmful to her. I know that one day when Nae-Nae has children of her own, that she will fully understand this, and all my decisions; and that she'll know that they were all made with her best interest at heart. I also know that a mother's love is fierce and will stop at nothing when it comes to her children. It's this love that kept me going; and that still today, keeps me going.

For a while, it was just Nae-Nae and I, the two of us, which was fine with me. My job was with the Army. When I wasn't at home with my daughter, I worked hard at my job with the goal to get ahead in life, not for myself so much, but for Nae-Nae. I wanted to give her everything and provide her with every opportunity that would make her life easier.

By the time Nae-Nae was eight years old, I got word that I'd have to deploy with my unit. The assignment was in Afghanistan. Since I'd previously had issues getting my daughter back into my custody when she'd been temporarily placed with Junior's parents, I made other arrangements for Nae-Nae's care before I shipped overseas.

It wasn't that I had anything against Junior's parents, but I wasn't entirely comfortable having Nae-Nae stay with them in Florida while I was stationed abroad. One time, after his sentencing, Junior's father had attempted a three-way call to connect Junior and me. I almost instantly hung up the phone and later told Junior's dad to never try something like that again. There was nothing I had to say to Junior and I wanted to keep him out of my life.

After a gut-wrenching goodbye with my daughter, I flew to Afghanistan to begin my assignment there. Jasima, a close friend whom I'd previously been stationed with in Korea, had a daughter who was a little older than Nae-Nae, so I trusted her to look after my daughter for me. When I deployed, it was November 2009.

While I worked in my Logistics job one day, I got a message. A staffer came into my office with a look of concern.

"Jas needs you to call her immediately! It's about Nae-Nae!"

"Isha!" Jasima said, as soon as she picked up her phone, "I don't know what's going on! I went to get Nae-Nae, and the school said she'd already been picked up!"

"What? By WHO?" I yelled as my heart nearly leapt from my chest.

"Something about her grandparents," Jas explained, "And a court order for temporary custody!"

"What? That's insane! What's going on? Oh, never mind! I'm calling the school right now!"

I hung up and dialed Nae-Nae's school.

"The principal please!" I said, as soon as a woman answered. "It's an emergency!"

When the principal answered, I barely let her get out a greeting before I interrupted.

"How did you let anyone take my daughter?" I demanded. "I am her mother and I didn't give permission for anyone to pick her up, except for Jasima, who's caring for her while I'm overseas! This is so irresponsible of you! Her grandparents are not her guardians!"

"Ma'am," the principal said, "Now, just calm down, please. The grandparents had an order of custody that was signed by a judge in Florida. We had to comply with it. It wasn't our choice."

"I'm not done with this!" I told the principal, as I hung up.

I raced to find my files with phone numbers and contact information. I found a paper with the number of the Clemency Board, so I called it, in hopes they would tell me that Junior was still in prison and had nothing to do with his parents going to a judge for custody of Nae-Nae.

"Oh, I'm sorry, ma'am," the woman on the phone said, "But your ex-husband was released a couple weeks ago. He is no longer incarcerated."

"What? He's not in prison right now?"

"No. It says right here that he's been released. I'm certain of it. Is there anything else I can help you with?"

I didn't even answer. I slowly hung-up the phone, and I felt like I'd been kicked in the stomach. I had been in Afghanistan for only a month and my world had been tossed upside-down without my knowledge of consent.

My heart felt like it might beat right out of my chest as I thought about how my daughter was probably with her father, the very man who'd taken my son from this Earth.

Nearly 7,500 miles away from my child, I felt helpless and scared. I also felt enraged and furious that Junior's parents had sneakily gone behind my back to a Florida judge.

But how does a judge take a woman's child from her custody when she's in the service and deployed on assignment in a foreign country? I wondered.

It didn't seem possible that it could have happened, and yet, it had. Once again, I couldn't eat, couldn't sleep and was plagued with worry as I petitioned the Army for emergency leave. My job as an Aviation Operations Specialist required rapt attention to detail, accuracy and quick thinking. Basically, my position meant I was charged with scheduling and dispatching tactical aircraft missions to help keep one of the largest fleets of aircraft in the world running safe and efficient. This meant processing local and cross-country flight clearances; checking the accuracy of flight plans and coordinating those plans; maintaining logs and records of incoming and outgoing flights; alerting crash crews in the event of emergencies; and monitoring weather reports that could mean the difference in success or failure of a mission, or even life and death, in some instances. In a nutshell, people's very lives sometimes depended on the abilities of persons in my position.

While I was usually on top of my game and pleasant to work with, as I waited for my leave to be approved, I felt helpless and miserable. I was trapped, across the world, and unable to reach my only child. The stress began to take its toll and I soon became easily agitated and quick-tempered. I even began cursing and behaving with hostility, possibly a result of lack of sleep; but nonetheless, it was an issue and I knew it.

"We're moving you to another office," my supervisor informed me. "It'll be better all the way around. Less stress, less responsibility, just while you're dealing with things."

I didn't care. I liked my job, but my mind was on my daughter. It was no secret. My focus wasn't one hundred percent where it usually was, and I welcomed the temporary change to a different, slower-paced office.

Chapter 9 – Choices

Just before Christmas, the Army granted my request for emergency leave. I returned home to the States to deal with Junior's parents and get my daughter back into my custody. The whole temporary custody thing had seemed insane to me; and I'd thought I would be able to simply return home and clear it all up.

I couldn't have been more wrong. I found it would take much more than a few phone calls to reverse what Junior's parents had somehow managed to do. To say it was a daunting tangle of red tape would be an understatement.

I called Junior's mom and let spew all the pent-up frustration and fury that had been brewing inside of me. She barely was able to get out a syllable as I let loose on her.

"How dare you!" I screamed into the phone. "You had no right! I am her mother!"

"We just did what's best for Nae-Nae," she interjected.

"*I* am her mother! *I* decide what's best for my daughter! You don't get to push your way into our lives and *take* my child! Who do you think you are?"

My next call was to an attorney. I requested that he start the paperwork necessary to regain custody of my daughter.

"We won't get a court date until August," the attorney explained.

"What? August?" I said. "That's eight months away! I want my daughter back where she belongs!"

"Listen," he said, as he tried to calm me, "I'm on your side. The courts are backlogged though, and that's just how it is."

Time passed painfully slowly as I waited for our court date for the custody hearing. To make matters worse, Junior's parents petitioned the court for permanent custody of Nae-Nae.

As the seasons changed, I tried to stay strong and hang on as I marked off the days on my calendar. I still mourned Ja and I missed Nae-Nae more than ever. It all seemed so unfair.

Haven't I been through enough? I thought. *When does it end?*

"Finally!" I said aloud, as I dressed on the morning of the August custody hearing.

I'd barely slept the night before and I couldn't wait to get to court. My resentment toward Junior's parents had grown in the months leading up to the custody hearing. I steeled myself as I walked into the courtroom alongside my attorney.

The courtroom wasn't what I'd expected. It seemed more informal than a typical courtroom. There was just a judge; Junior's parents and their attorney; and my attorney and myself. Both attorneys addressed the judge and he asked multiple questions.

"I've reviewed the temporary custody order," the judge said, "And even I am befuddled as to how it came into being. Nonetheless, here we are today."

My back relaxed the least little bit and I allowed myself a deep, cleansing breath, hopeful that the judge understood my position. My attorney patted my forearm, as the judge continued.

"Upon review of all the facts and the documentation, I am reversing the temporary order of custody. Permanent custody shall be awarded to the biological mother of the minor child."

Tears welled in my eyes and a lump formed in my throat as I gratefully gasped. Junior's parents sighed and shifted in their seats, obviously irritated and disappointed by the judge's ruling.

"But," the judge continued, "The minor child will spend time, one weekend each month, with her grandparents."

This was the arrangement, years earlier, after Ja had died. Junior's parents had been allowed visitation one weekend per month but I was the permanent custodial parent and legal guardian for my daughter.

"The minor child is to be returned to her mother's custody on Friday," the judge declared.

My head began to spin. I was thrilled that Nae-Nae was coming home, but I was expected to fly back to Afghanistan on Sunday. This meant, that after all the months of waiting for the custody hearing, I would have less than two days with my daughter before I was to ship out again.

As soon as we walked out of the courtroom, I called my command. I was hopeful that someone would understand my desperate plight. After all, I'd put in nine and a half years with the Army, including active duty and time in the Reserves.

Surely, that'll count for something, I thought, as the phone rang in my ear.

I was transferred to the rear D Sergeant Major at the Hunter Army Airfield in Savannah. He listened as I explained what had occurred in the past months and how I have to fight to regain custody of my daughter after what had happened with her grandparents.

"I understand," he finally said. "I also see that you were granted emergency leave to deal with your situation."

"Yes, sir," I confirmed. "That's correct."

"I'm afraid there's nothing more the Army can do at this time," he explained.

"So, I'm supposed to have less than two days with my daughter and then fly off and leave her? How can I do that?"

"Well, if you don't get on that plane and return to Afghanistan," he said, "We will start the paperwork to separate you from the Army."

Once again, that familiar 'sucker-punched feeling' hit me as I tried to digest what I'd just heard.

"After nearly 10 years of service, this is what I get?" I asked.

"I'm afraid so."

There wasn't even an option. I didn't have to think about it.

"Then let's start that paperwork," I said.

It felt like he'd made it clear that I had to choose between the Army and my only remaining child. There was no other answer. There was only one choice. After all the paperwork had been completed, I was honorably discharged on September 26 from the Army.

Chapter 10 – A Mother's Love

With my daughter back in my arms, and fully in my custody, life felt good again and better than it had in a long time. She and I had always been especially close; and by now, Nae-Nae was going on nine years old and she was simply a joy to be around. We laughed and talked all the time, snuggled in front of the TV, went to movies and to the mall; and spent nearly all our time together.

I loved to wake up in the mornings, help Nae-Nae get ready and then put her on the school bus to begin her day. Nothing was sweeter than seeing my daughter's smiling face as she waved to me from the bus window after she took her seat. Later in the afternoon, I routinely met the school bus when it returned Nae-Nae each day after school. We both looked forward to the afternoons when she got home from school.

"Mommy," Nae-Nae often said, with a big grin, "I'm so glad to have you here!"

"And I am happy to BE here!" I always replied, before I hugged her.

It was all so normal. I enjoyed the typical, ordinary, and simplest of things with my daughter. Years before, I'd never dreamt that I would ever again feel happy and content, but I was just that. My heart was full and I was happy, *genuinely happy*. One day, as I watched Nae-Nae as she did her homework, I realized that another little piece of my heart had finally healed.

My son was always in my heart, but the pain wasn't as bad by this time; and I could think of Ja and remember him in happier times, as I recalled his smiling face and infectious laughter. It was as if his memory strengthened me and propelled me forth in my life so I could be the mother to Nae-Nae that she deserved.

While it wasn't up to my daughter to make me happy, just being with her did that alone. I was so grateful for the bond we'd built and the life we had together; and I couldn't imagine that it was possible to love a child more than I loved my own. After a while, I felt like it was time for a little more.

Before my deployment, I had started to date a bit and I eventually met a guy who became more special than the rest, so he and I saw each other exclusively. He was in the Army, so he and I had that in common too. Prior to going to court for the custody hearing over Nae-Nae, Todd and I got engaged. Following the day when the court had returned my daughter to my custody, Todd, Nae-Nae and I lived together.

We were living in Hinesville, a small town in Georgia that's located near Fort Stewart. I didn't particularly like Hinesville though. With a population of about 30,000, it was a little too slow for me. It's a quaint coastal town, with

Spanish moss hanging from live oak trees and history all around; and there are families who've been in town for many generations. There are various museums in Hinesville, state parks and a typical 'small town USA' feeling all around. But, as a girl who'd grown up in New Jersey, quickly grew a bit restless for something more than what Hinesville offered.

"I know you're not really happy here," Todd said one day. "What would you think about moving to Oklahoma?"

"What?" I laughed. "Oklahoma? What's in Oklahoma?"

"Well, I will be," he said. "I got put on orders today and that's where I'll be going."

I had no idea what to expect in Oklahoma, but it sounded as equally slow

137

and stagnant as Hinesville to me. Also, since Todd and I weren't married, I wasn't thrilled about the prospect of uprooting Nae-Nae and moving us to a new place.

"I know what you're thinking," Todd said. "So, let's get married. I mean, we're already engaged; we were planning to get married anyway. Let's do it now."

We got married at the Justice of the Peace office in Hinesville and I began to pack up our house and our belongings in preparation for the upcoming move. Nae-Nae was fine with the idea of moving, since she'd be with Mommy. That's all that mattered to her.

It was November when we arrived in Oklahoma. I knew the state was rugged and somewhat rocky, with small mountain ranges, mesas, prairies and some forests; but I kept thinking *What is there to **do** in Oklahoma?'*

Todd and I found a nice home in a comfortable neighborhood, located off the Army base in town. We moved in, got unpacked and it was time for Thanksgiving.

I enrolled Nae-Nae in school and tried to acclimate to our new hometown; and before I knew it, Christmas was upon us. We'd begun to settle in to our typical family dynamic.

Todd and Nae-Nae had a good relationship, and for that, I was grateful. But the relationship between Todd and I was a different story. It's probably because we married to soon and then had the strain of the move, but he and I were truly miserable as a couple. We were both negative all the time, and Todd seemed constantly angry with me. He and I could find a reason to argue about anything and everything, it seemed. Neither of us was acclimating well to Oklahoma or to being married.

Although Todd was good to Nae-Nae, my daughter got upset with him when he yelled at me during our arguments. She was very defensive and protective of her mom. This tense dynamic went on for nearly a year, and I knew something had to change.

As much as I loved being the proverbial 'wife and mother,' and being there for Nae-Nae, I knew that I needed to get back to work if I were to leave my unhealthy marriage. Once again, I was forced to take a hard look at life and make more choices.

Chapter 11 – The New Beginning

"No!" Nae-Nae protested. "I don't want you to go back to the Army!"

"But Mommy has to go to work where the money is, so I can make the best money to take care of us," I explained.

The conversation wasn't going well; and it was pretty much just what I'd expected.

I didn't want to leave my daughter any more than she wanted me to go, but the training I'd received in the Army made it possible for me to look overseas for better employment positions that paid more.

"Listen, Honey," I explained further. "It's not exactly the Army. I'll be working in the same place where I worked when I was in the Army, but I'll be working for a company."

"But will you have to carry a gun, Mommy?"

"No," I assured her. "And I'll only work there for a year."

"You'll probably do two years," my intuitive daughter sighed, as she shook her head, looking much wiser than her nearly nine years.

Todd and I had both come to realize we needed to let our marriage go. It was clear that it would never work, no matter how we tried. Our parting was amicable and I only wish him well in his life.

In the past year, Junior's parents and I had achieved a good, respectful relationship and they saw Nae-Nae when they could. Although I didn't care for how they'd gone about gaining temporary custody of my daughter, there was never a question of their love for their grandchild. For this reason, I made plans for Nae-Nae to finish out the school year and then go and stay in Florida with her grandparents.

Because of my Army training, I looked for a job working in logistics for a contractor, which would utilize skills while also earning a good salary. My security   clearance, however, was nearing its expiration date; and so I knew I had to take any overseas job that was available and that would utilize my security credentials, which were considered to be valuable by employers. I found, and was quickly hired for, a job with the post office in Afghanistan. It was far from my ideal position, but I knew it would get me to where I wanted to go, so I viewed the job as a steppingstone on the path toward my ultimate goal.

In September 2011, I said a painful goodbye to Nae-Nae, with the promise to talk with her and visit frequently face-to-face via Skype and FaceTime. Only the lump in my throat matched the one in my chest as I hugged my daughter and breathed in her scent to commit it to memory.

"And remember," Nae-Nae reminded me. "No guns!"

About 15 hours later, my plane touched down again on Afghanistan sand. I'll admit that it was incredibly difficult to leave my daughter, but I knew I'd never earn the same money in the States that I could soon earn overseas. It was all part of my plan; and so once again, I dug deep and drew on my newfound strength to take the next steps for my daughter's future. I looked at Nae-Nae and Ja's photos one more time, before I deplaned and breathed in the arid air of Afghanistan and felt the hot sun on my face.

You've got this, I reminded myself.

During the first three weeks at my post office job, I worked the nightshift; and I sent out resumes during the daytime. In less than

145

a month, I was hired to be a Movement Control Specialist in the Logistics Department of a private company that contracted services to the US Army. So, once again, I was working *with* the Army, but not *for* the Army; and I was earning a great salary.

If not for the money, I doubt too many people would sign-up for a contracting job overseas. Our employer, as part of our compensation package, provides housing for their employees. It's nothing elaborate, by any standards though. Employees share quarters that are set-up similar to dorm housing, with lightweight partitions separating private spaces. Since employees work round the clock, people come and go at all hours, but it's something everyone gets used to, since there's not much that can be done about it.

"Awww!" a co-worker said, as she nodded toward the two photos near my computer one day. "Are those your kids?"

"Yeah," I smiled. "Nae-Nae and Ja."

"They're both adorable!"

"They are!" I agree. "Thank you!"

It's true. I have two children, both of whom I always carry in my heart, but only one that I can also hold in my arms. That'll never change, although *I've* grown and changed so much in the past few years. I am blessed with the love of my beautiful daughter, fueled by my passion for life and strengthened by Ja's memory.

EPILOGUE

An epilogue is meant to deliver a kind of finality and to be an ending of sorts, but my story continues; and even *I* do not know the ending. I don't want to know the ending though. Today, I'm enjoying the journey, since I've learned so much about myself.

In the last few years, I've learned many things. While there was once a time that I couldn't imagine how I'd possibly take another step, much less take even another breath, after getting through the loss of my son, I am today a confident, strong survivor. I've learned that there is indeed life after such a horrific, life-altering loss.

Tragedies affect us, but they do not define us. I'm not *just* 'the mom whose son has died.' I'm so much more; and I'm even things that I have yet to discover about myself.

We are not a prisoner of 'our stories,' our lives and our stories do go on. While 'our stories' are certainly forever a part of us, they are just that: a *part* of us, a part of the ultimate person we will become, once we've made it to the other side of the darkness that had once threatened to swallow us whole.

My son is today in every breath I take, and every decision I make; but my daughter is my main focus. Her happiness and success in life is my main objective. It's what she deserves, and anything less would mean that I've failed her as her mother. My daughter deserves to be surrounded by love, embraced by people who value her and want the best for her. She is, to me, like a vessel that I must fill with only goodness, happiness, laughter and love.

As she matures, my goal is to let my daughter learn from my trials and my triumphs. While I hope she never has to face the sadness or hardships that I have known, it is my job to prepare her to know that she can navigate and leap over any hurdle in her path. She has in her a kind of wisdom and a grace that will serve her well. Coupled with her maturity, intelligence and beauty, she's got so much going for her already.

My hope is that my daughter witnesses my strength, and acknowledges her own; but much earlier than I did, and without going down the path that I was forced to travel. Most parents want the best for their kids, and they want to 'give their kids the world' and to 'make life easier' for their children than their own has been. This includes myself; but I also want to impart in my daughter an inner confidence and an impenetrable strength that'll serve her well throughout life.

As it turned out, and of little surprise to those who know her best, Nae-Nae was correct when she said I would 'be in Afghanistan for more than a year.' Perhaps my intuitive daughter knows me better than I know myself, at times!

My main focus is today, and has always been in being Nae-Nae's mother, teaching and guiding her and raising her to be a strong, independent woman. I am currently trying to find a nice home for us located in a good neighborhood within a great school district. Nae-Nae continues to excel in her advanced placement classes and has always been an A-student. While she continues to learn about her world, my daughter also brings so much love and light into mine!

I am forever blessed to be the mother of both of my children; as my story continues.

Made in the USA
Columbia, SC
02 August 2020